Free E-Book!!!

As a "thank you" to
πNautilus readers, a free
E-Book copy of
πNautilus Guide for
Personal Navigation is
available at:

free.piNautilus.com

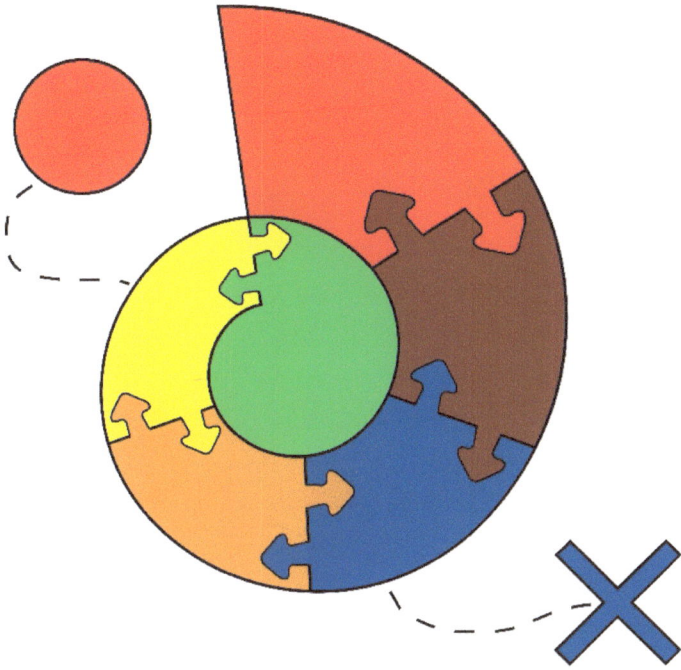

πNautilus™

Guide for Personal Navigation

Eric K. Beschinski

ISBN: 978-1-7356051-4-2 (Paperback)

ISBN: 978-1-7356051-5-9 (E-Book)

Library of Congress Control Number: 2020922728

Images and artwork by Eric Beschinski.

Book design by Eric Beschinski.

Printed by Kindle Direct Publishing a division of Amazon, Inc., in the United States of America.

First printing edition 2020.

Published by:

Greenfire Innovations, LLC
2700 Valparaiso St. #1041
Valparaiso, IN 46384

CONTENTS

Acknowledgments

I am pretty sure my wife is my biggest fan. Jenny is ridiculously supportive of me and my endeavors. Honestly, I would not want to walk this road with anyone else. She is my partner in life, work, and spirit. I am thankful every day that God blessed me with such an amazing woman to call my wife.

My gratitude for this book and methodology extends to others as well. Specifically, I want to thank Courtney Smith who was my first coaching client (aka guinea pig). Not only did this help me further refine the iNautilus methodology and help me find gaps in application, but her engagement and enthusiastic participation provided invaluable experience coaching a business owner. In addition, working through those early sessions with Courtney showed me how important it was to release πNautilus Guide for Personal Navigation, the "prequal" to the iNautilus Guide for Organizational Navigation. As we focused on her law firm, the need to identify her own Ideal Destination was instrumental in releasing πNautilus when I did.

I want to thank my pre-launch team, my other clients, all of the friends and associates who have been on this voyage with me (even if they didn't know it at the time). It's exciting to create new things, and I'm glad you were there with me through the process.

Finally, I want to mention my stepson, Evan (he's 9), simply because he wanted to be in my next book. Thanks for being a good kid and letting me marry your mom, Evan.

Chapter 1: The End

Per the wise recommendation of Stephen Covey in his famous book, *The 7 Habits of Highly Effective People*.[1], I am beginning with the end in mind. The entire purpose of this methodology is The End. There are many personal/business books on the shelves with lots of different tools, ideas, and structures. While the πNautilus encompasses strategic planning, it is not a strategic planning methodology. Although the πNautilus encompasses execution, it is not an execution strategy. Strategic planning is stationary, but Navigation is strategy in motion. The πNautilus is an integrated system that will help you get from where you are to where you want to be. And that is The End to which I am referring.

Please do not misunderstand. The End is not really the end. It is merely an endpoint. Like T.S. Elliot said, "What we call the beginning is often the end. And to make an end is to make a beginning. The end is where we start from." So, this is a rolling methodology that will help define that desired endpoint but allows for detours and/or changes of course along the way. Navigation.

This whole idea originated from a need I saw. While I was researching and building a training model for leaders in 2007, I realized that there is a lot of information about strategic planning and goal execution, but

---

[1] <u>The 7 Habits of Highly Effective People</u> by Stephen Covey, Free Press a Division of Simon & Schuster, Inc., Copyright © 2004

there was nothing that tied it all together. There was no visual from which to work. There was no system. Shortly thereafter, I envisioned the Nautilus. It is a spiral found in nature, often approximating the Golden ratio[2]. The mathematical implications really had nothing to do with it… The spiral shape allows for sequence and direction while also keeping all the components directly connected (as you can see on the cover and throughout the book).

After years of struggling to provide clear definitions and articulate why my definition for key terms needed to be used when working with the Nautilus, I finally had the realization that I needed to break free from the terminology that has been used, misused, poorly defined, and jumbled together. Then I applied a theme and created new terms that I could define. Thus, Nautilus was reborn as iNautilus (Integrated Nautilus). The iNautilus is the framework for Organizational Navigation and leads naturally to the πNautilus (Personal Integrated Nautilus). While you will likely recognize similarities between the pieces of the πNautilus and the concepts of core values, mission statements, vision statements, and goals, it is important that with the new framework of the πNautilus comes a fresh perspective on the words and ideas involved. Each chapter will introduce a piece of the πNautilus. Order is important as well (another hurdle I struggled to overcome when using more traditional terminology). So, this book will explain the Personal Integrity Compass (πComp), Personal Identity Map (πMap), Personal Ideal Destination (πDest), Personal Indicator Points (πPoints), Personal Incremental Routes (πRoutes), and Personal Immediate Tasks (πTasks).

You may struggle a bit with the fact that this new terminology often overlaps more traditional vocabulary, but I assure you that it is necessary. There is inherent difficulty trying to convince anyone to adopt πNautilus-specific definitions for core values, mission, vision, and goals. Re-learning is much harder than learning. I also did not want anyone to feel that I was

---

[2] The Golden ratio, closely related to the Fibonacci sequence, refers to a series of numbers where each number is the sum of the 2 preceding numbers (0, 1, 1, 2, 3, 5, 8, 13, 21 and so on). When expressed geometrically as a series of squares with those numbers as the dimensions of the sides, a spiral pattern emerges. It is this pattern that is often approximated in nature (galaxies, storms, flower petals, leaf patterns, pine cone structure, and shells like that of the nautilus.)

telling them their definitions for these ideas (or their mission/vision statements) were "wrong". Rather, a set of new words with new definitions put in the "correct" order **according to the framework of the πNautilus** circumvents the issue. It is cleaner and allows us to progress through the methodology with less conflict from previously learned strategic planning models.

The πNautilus is a paradigm shift in the way life strategy is approached, and it defines, clarifies, and unifies the principles of mission, vision, and values in a way never done before. Furthermore, the πNautilus is a model that provides a visual representation of the concepts so that they are clear and functional. While there is nothing revolutionary about the underlying concepts, the methodology is structured in a way that is systematic, visual, and easy to replicate. That **is** revolutionary, and I am excited to begin sharing the πNautilus with you.

Proverbs 29:18 - "Where there is no vision, the people perish…" (KJV)

Eric K. Beschinski

Chapter 2: Vacation Analogy

Although I have no seafaring experience, nautical concepts like compasses, maps, and others have provided a useful framework for the ideas in πNautilus. Similarly, planning a vacation provides a useful analogy for getting from point A to point B.

I will be breaking down the Vacation Analogy into a series of steps. Often, when planning a vacation some of these steps are intermingled or overlap. However, in reality they are distinct processes. When planning a vacation, the same types of steps are followed as when planning a life-long dream.

So, the first step is to determine what is important to you and your family while vacationing. Relaxation? Fun? New Experiences? Culture? This list would be like your family's vacation core values. You may not be able to accomplish all of these in a single vacation, but it is vital to know what you value. What you value will help define your purpose.

That brings us to the next step, determining the primary objective of this vacation (the mission so to speak). Do you want to relax, soak up some sun, and maybe read a little? Would you rather see some of the amazing beauties of creation? How about an amusement park extravaganza for the whole family? What you want to accomplish with this particular vacation is a crucial step. If you skip this step, you are much more likely to be disappointed with your trip. Defining that purpose for a vacation is fairly simple (unless you have a disagreement between the interested parties).

Then, with that purpose in mind, you need to select a destination. Where does your family want to go? Skipping the first 2 steps above makes this step harder and more likely to disappoint. If you want to relax in the sun on a beach, Disney World may not be the best destination. Conversely, if you have kids, lounging on the beach is probably going to get boring for them after the first few hours (or minutes). The destination can be determined (or at least some destinations can be ruled out) by clearly understanding the purpose. Another aspect of this step is timeframe. If you know when you want to go, then you have a "deadline" which may further clarify your destination options.

Once you choose a "where" and "when", now there are travel plans. How are you going to get there? Flying? Driving? If you are driving for example, are there some sights along the way you might want to visit? Even if not, there are clear markers that will help you benchmark your progress toward the destination (cities, states, landmarks, etc.)

Then of course, there is the itinerary or route (logistics). If you are flying then you need to determine flights, transportation to/from airports, rental car, hotels, and more. If you are driving, then it is all about the route you plan to take, stops along the way, and hotels.

Finally, there are all the checklists and plans for saving, packing, preparation plus successful departure, travel, and arrival at the destination.

All of this is usually done through conversation when planning a vacation. Although you may never have jotted down your "vacation core values", I would be quite surprised if you had difficulty doing so. Although most of us would not break down the vacation planning process to this level of detail, it should be evident that the methodology is similar to planning a "life destination". The major difference is in scale. The process is abbreviated for a family vacation since that type of planning is simpler, has a shorter life cycle, and is less critical.

While the analogy risks oversimplifying the process, it genuinely helps to provide a more concrete and comprehensible lens through which to focus on the underlying concepts.

Chapter 3: Big Red Dot

P rior to diving into the πNautilus, there is a preliminary process that needs some attention. You must identify your Big Red Dot. This is the "you are here" dot on a map. It is your starting point. Before you can determine where you want to go OR how to get there, it is essential to know where you are.

Imagine if you and your family are kidnapped, blindfolded, and dropped off in the woods many hours, maybe days later. You will probably want to go home. But at that moment, not knowing where you are, every step you take is more likely taking you further from home, not closer. You must first figure out where you are.

OK, so you are PROBABLY not lost in the woods. Nevertheless, you must define your Big Red Dot before doing anything else. This is not about where you want to go (that comes later). Rather, it is about clearly articulating your state of existence right now.

Defining your Big Red Dot is not that difficult. It is a statement of the status quo. Ask yourself things like:

- What words define me?
- What am I contributing to the world or my community right now?
- Who am I? Who would others say I am? Who would God say I am?
- What do I believe about myself? What is the truth about those beliefs?
- What are my "stats"?
- Where am I right now (in life)?

Include pertinent information about who you are (characteristics, skills, strengths, weaknesses), what you do (work, leisure, service), who you influence and how far you reach with that influence, meaningful numbers (think quantifiable data like age, income, family size, etc.), and anything else you "see" around you that helps identify your present state. The Big Red Dot is a "state of the self" address. And while your core identity is part of your Big Red Dot, do not confuse who you are with where you are or what you do.

The first sentence of your Big Red Dot is what I call your Core Identity. As challenging as it might be at first, clearly define who you are in one sentence. This is NOT about what you have, what you do, what you have done, or what others say about you. Your Core Identity is discovered internally, planted there by God. Simply put, you are who He says you are. If you take time to explore that with Him, He will show you your Core Identity. The rest of your Big Red Dot can address other aspects of where you are in life, but reserve that first sentence for your Core Identity.

There is a guide at the back of this book to help you. Please identify your Big Red Dot before proceeding. Doing so will help clarify the rest of the πNautilus as you progress through it.

Throughout this book, these principles will be put into practice in a very tangible way. As you progress through the πNautilus, I will be openly sharing my own voyage. So, below is my Big Red Dot™:

Eric Beschinski is a child of God, Christ-follower, husband, father, entrepreneur, and author; he was designed in God's image to exhibit intelligence, passion, strength, and diligence*. Right now, he is in a planning/building phase, impacting the world through writing, business coaching, and small contributions to his church and non-profits. At 45 years old, his family is a complex tapestry. While his kids are transitioning due to ages/stages of life, his parents are doing well with retirement, and his grandparents' health is starting to deteriorate. Eric maintains his own physical health by continuing to lose weight, playing volleyball twice per week, and lifting weights weekly. In addition:

- *He is building a consulting business from scratch, promoting and coaching the iNautilus, organizational navigation, sales, and entrepreneurship.*
- *He and Jenny have a nice home in Valparaiso that will soon be too large (as the kids move out on their own), and they own 2 rental properties. Most of Eric's more important possessions*

(cars, computers, etc.) are older models and/or lessor-quality versions.

- *Eric has mostly recovered from his divorce, although the financial ramifications continue for now. His relationship with his wife, Jenny, is strong and loving. However, there are challenges with Eric's kids, all of whom are adults (or will be very soon).*

*Core Identity is in bold

πComp

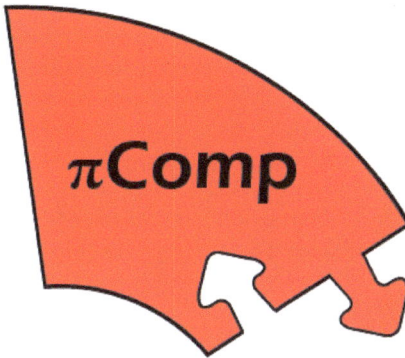

Chapter 4: Personal Integrity Compass

Core values are perhaps the most significantly underrated point of reference for people and organizations. In addition to identifying what you view as important, non-negotiable truth, "Core values are ideals that guide personal or institutional choices" (Smith & Lindsay 95).[3]. Authors Smith & Lindsay go on to say, "Rarely does a person or organization compromise Core Values without long-term damage" (97)[2]. It is crucial that leaders, from the one-man-show general contractor to the Fortune 500 employee, take the time to clearly define his or her core values.

In order to help you do that in the πNautilus way, the Personal Integrity Compass is comprised of 4 to 8 Cardinal Directives. These Cardinal Directives should:

- Steer the strategic process
- Identify what you view as important, non-negotiable truth
- Define key indicators
- Lay the foundation for everything else

---

[3] Leading Change In Your World by Mark A. Smith and Larry M. Lindsay, Triangle Publishing, Copyright © 2001

So, it is naturally by design that the πComp is at the top of the πNautilus. It represents the apex and the starting point. In addition, the πComp is colored red for specific reasons; it is the lifeblood of the process.

Figure 1

Red is often associated with emotions and the πComp is emotion driven. Red usually symbolizes excitement, energy, love, desire, strength, power, sincerity, and all things intense and passionate. Even in a "cold, calculating" organized strategy system, I contend the Heart must come first. Passion and love are the reasons most dreams are ever dreamed in the first place. Of course, it would be irresponsible to ignore the relationship between the color red and a stop sign… in other words, go no further in this process (other than finishing reading the book) until you have your πComp on paper. There is a πComp Worksheet provided in the back of the book to help guide you. (Oh, and cardinals are red too.)

Since the πComp reflects the personal core values of leaders, it only stands to reason that these same principles carry forward into the organizations they lead. Working through the πNautilus will provide clarity for the related system of Organizational Navigation, the iNautilus. This usually is not too difficult. Often, these Cardinal Directives are concepts that leaders have rolling around in their minds constantly but have never taken the time to put down on paper. Take that time as soon as you have finished this book. You must identify what you value before you can determine what to do with that information (and before you can define what you want your organization to value). Organizational ideology is usually a projection of the leader's ideals, and that is a good thing. (The iNautilus Guide for Organizational Navigation provides this strategy + execution model for companies, non-profits, and churches to implement.)

Now that the πComp is defined, here are some parameters for extracting yours:

- Determine a manageable number while being comprehensive (usually four to eight Cardinal Directives)
- Ask very simply, "What do I value most? In myself? In others?

- Identify each with a one to three-word key phrase
- For a clearer πComp, include an adjective in the Cardinal Directive
- Elaborate on each if they need further clarification

Some examples that help demonstrate effective Cardinal Directives include:

- Green Practices – Proactively minimizing my environmental footprint and promoting recycling
- Honesty – Dealing honestly with everyone
- Abundance Mentality – Realizing that opportunities abound, and possibilities are endless
- Community – My neighborhood/city/region is part of my home and also my responsibility
- Creative Frugality.ₘ[4]
- Respectful Compassion[3]

Notice the power of adding a descriptive word before the concept… Consider the difference between "Frugality" and "Creative Frugality". This is by no means a requirement, but it does give some added emphasis, greater clarity, and better decision-steering ability to the Cardinal Directives in the πComp.

Of course, these are merely examples of some possible Cardinal Directives. Do not make the mistake of feeling that you must list everything you value. The idea is to clearly define your CORE values, the (few) ideals you value above everything else. It may not be easy, but it is absolutely vital.

One other key point to make about the πComp: always place the most important Cardinal Directive at the top. This is your True North.

Continuing to lead by example, my Cardinal Directives are:

- *Consistent Integrity - which encompasses honesty, ethics, reputation, and wholeness (my True North)*

---

[4] These are the core values of the City of Valparaiso, Indiana restated as nouns instead of adjectives. According to the Strategic Plan of the city (http://www.ci.valparaiso.in.us/DocumentCenter/View/946/Strategic-plan-final-4-9-09?bidId=), the values are Honestly Accountable, Surprisingly Responsive, Creatively Frugal, Respectfully Compassionate, and Boldly Proactive.

- *Honor - treating others' as special, doing more than is expected, and having a positive attitude.[5]*
- *Community - being involved locally with the public and organizations*
- *Helping Others - improving the lives of individuals*
- *Justice - ensuring that moral rightness (according to God's standards) prevails, especially when it comes to fighting the exploitation of people*
- *Sincerity - meaning what one says and saying what one means*
- *Excellence - abolishing apathy and mediocrity*
- *Passionate Conviction - faith and belief that is evident by action*

Just like a compass rose on a map clearly orients the viewer to the landscape, the πComp orients yourself in the landscape of life.

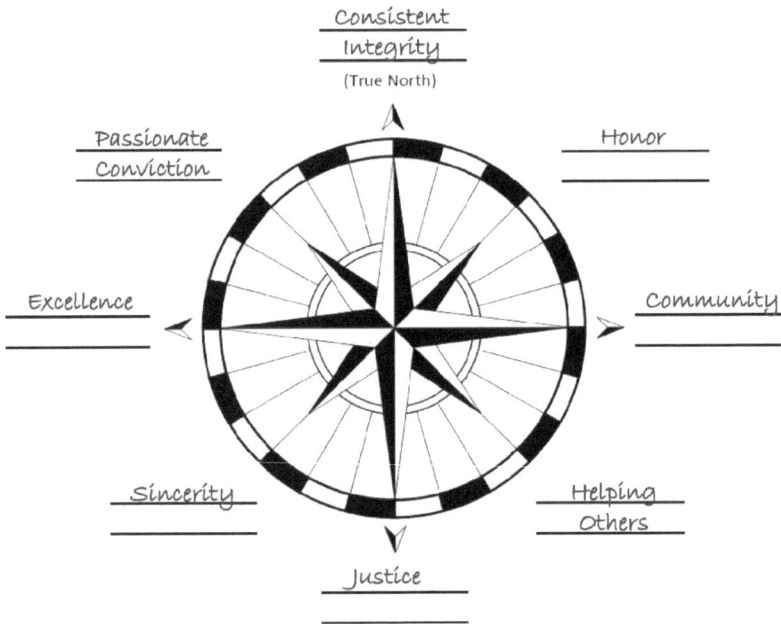

---

[5] This is the definition of "honor" provided by authors Scott Turansky and Joanne Miller in their book, Say Goodbye to Whining, Complaining, and Bad Attitudes... in You and Your Kids, WaterBook Press, Copyright © 2000

πMap

Chapter 5: Personal Identity Map

The Personal Identity Map can be defined in one word: "purpose". It is the purpose you exist to fulfill. More succinctly, the πMap explains <u>why</u> you are here. Depending on your religious beliefs and/or worldview this may be easier or harder for you to verbalize. However, I know many people with a strong faith-based existence who have wrestled with their own purpose, so faith is no guarantee of an easy answer. You need to have something you want to be <u>about</u>. This is something really big. Too big to be measured. So big, in fact, that if it is ever fully accomplished, your time on this planet is at its end. Your πMap is perpetual and should not be "complete-able". An example might help clarify. Consider the following:

I exist to cure the world of cancer. Or…

My purpose in life is to ensure that every orphan has a warm bed, clean clothing, and plenty of food.

With those examples in mind, if you ever completely fulfilled either of those, there would be no reason to continue working. If cancer has been eradicated, mission accomplished. All the orphans are cared for… now what? Even though it is extremely unlikely that a single person is going to solve problems of this magnitude, either is still a valid πMap.

Further, your purpose is not something that changes every few years. If it changes at all, it should change very slowly over time (decades). Of course, there are always exceptions. Many God-followers would refer to this iMap as a "calling". If God is calling you to one purpose, He just might call you to a different purpose 5 years from now. That is not a problem. Just define your new iMap and work through the πNautilus from there. Be careful not to confuse a purpose with a destination... I believe that we were all created for a purpose, and while God can change that purpose mid-stream if He chooses to do so, that is not the norm. Usually, your purpose exists from the moment you are born to the day you die.

It is of great importance and value to clearly define the purpose for your existence. Not only does this provide a tangible means of communicating said purpose both internally and externally, but it becomes a mechanism by which to filter actions and decisions. You would not, for example, begin a non-profit to end world hunger if your calling is to battle cancer. That sounds absurd, but many people do similar (if less exaggerated) things every day. If a significant action (maybe any action) does not help to fulfill your mission, it should have no part in your life. That is a divisive statement, but it needs to be said.

Examples abound of people lacking purpose. The friends who live to work and accumulate wealth or "toys" (I'm not saying there is anything wrong with wealth) might lack purpose. Family members who struggle with career choices or hop from job to job might simply be struggling to know and understand their calling. Many people operate without a clear purpose defining why they exist <u>at all</u>, why they exist <u>where they are</u> (instead of another community, another city, another state, or another country), what sets them apart from the other people (without this, there is no clear answer to why they are needed and uniquely gifted), and what God desires from them (which is always what they are perfectly designed to accomplish). Americans are highly prone to apathy and mediocrity. People often assume that "someone else will take care of that." Unfortunately, that often simply means that no one is taking care of it (or too few are doing so).

In the Vacation Analogy we are now at the step of determining the primary objective of the vacation.

In the same way a map provides a birds-eye, big-picture view of a geographical area, the Personal Identity Map provides a high-level view of your purpose. And like a map has a legend to explain some of the map details to the viewer, you need a Legend Statement™ to clearly articulate your purpose. The πMap in the πNautilus is brown which commonly represents Earth, stability, reliability, comfort, endurance, and simplicity… appropriate for an Identity Map.

A Legend Statement is a "living document" which should verbalize your Personal Integrity Compass (Cardinal Directives) and Personal Identity Map. In order to form your Legend Statement, here are the types of questions you should ask yourself:

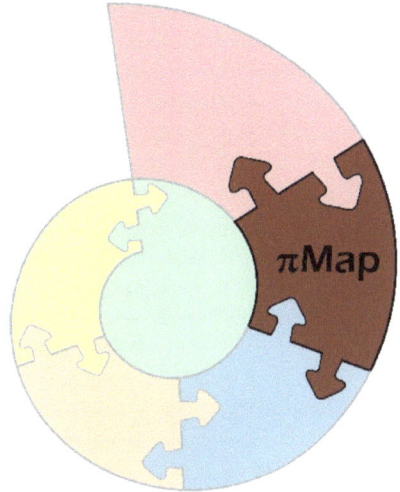

Figure 2

- What do I value?
- What is my True North?
- Why do I exist?
- What distinguishes me from others?
- Why am I in this location?
- What is my primary objective?

State the purpose (πMap) and incorporate the Cardinal Directives (πComp). See the Legend Statement guide at the back of the book. Again, in the spirit of leading by example, here is my Legend Statement:

> God created me to help others fulfill their purpose. He designed me with a desire to learn, solve problems, and make the world better. My battle is against apathy, mediocrity, and injustice; my affinity for public speaking, coaching, and training helps me to inspire others to be better and show them ways to grow. I am a Christ-follower who values honoring and helping people through relationship and community. In addition, I am passionate about strong conviction, justice, and sincerity. I strive for excellence in everything. But consistent integrity is paramount, my True North, and I expect the same in others.

Eric K. Beschinski

Chapter 6: Personal Ideal Destination

Once the πComp is defined and the πMap is understood (and only after these are clearly stated "on paper" in a Legend Statement), a Personal Ideal Destination can develop. The concept of πDest is often made unnecessarily complicated. Essentially, a πDest is a massive, long-term goal. Some have dubbed the idea a BHAG (Big, Hairy, Audacious Goal)[6]. Most have a general understanding of what a goal is and what it looks like, and that will suffice.

If the purpose of the vacation is an example of the πMap, then πDest is the destination. Just like planning a vacation, a πDest has a specific & unique identity, a planned route to get there, an estimated arrival date/time, and everyone involved knows when you have arrived.

Without a pre-defined purpose (πMap and by extension πComp), you can still pick a destination for your trip. However, if you choose your destination based on your desired purpose, your vacation will be much more rewarding, fulfilling, and... well... purposeful. The same goes for your πDest. It is definitely possible to cast a vision for your life without a mission

---

[6] From <u>Built to Last: Successful Habits of Visionary Companies</u> by James Collins and Jerry Porras, William Collins (Publisher), Copyright © 1994

in place or without core values, but then the questions arise, "Why am I going there?" and even worse, "Why am I going anywhere at all?"

OK, that's enough about the order of events. Can you imagine planning a vacation without choosing a destination in advance? "Let's get in the car, kids, we're going somewhere, and we won't be back for two weeks." Imagine the questions… "Where are we going? What kind of clothes should we pack? What are we going to do? How much money should we bring? What about…? How are we…?" For most of us, that would be absurd. Unfortunately, many people operate this way every day. Either they have no destination, so they go nowhere, or they make an attempt to move forward, grow, and change without ever really knowing/planning where they are going.

Determining a πDest for yourself is no small task either, but it can be incredibly fun and exciting. It feels good to know the Cardinal Directives, understand the πMap, and have a πDest to guide you into the future. The object is to paint a word-picture of your life in 5 to 10 years. This needs to be as specific as possible. If your vacation destination is Florida, that is not very helpful. Florida is a big state and there are many things to do there. Regardless of your vacation purpose, you can probably find a destination that would align with it. In order to have an effective πDest, details are necessary. "We are going to stay at Disney's Contemporary Resort at the Magic Kingdom in Disney World, Orlando, FL from February 18th through February 25th, 2022." That is a pretty precise description. Add a room number and 1) anyone could send you a package, 2) you can Google a route to fly/drive there, 3) you know when you expect to get there, and 4) the whole family will know when you have finally arrived.

Your πDest is a piece of your Ideal Existence as a human being. Imagine your life filled with joy and peace, free from worry and striving. Although the Ideal Existence may not be fully realized this side of eternity, we have been given enough goodness to be able to imagine a perfect life. There are six components to Ideal Existence, and all of these should be addressed in your πDest. The six components are grouped into 1) a healthy human (body, mind, & soul) and 2) healthy being (relationships, finances, and time).

Focusing internally, the "human" aspects involve ensuring the future health of your physical body, improving your mind, and nourishing your soul. For your body, envision a healthy body and the actions that lead to and maintain that body such as what you eat and how you exercise. To improve your mind, consider adding knowledge, wisdom, and experiences. Reading more, for example, is a common way to grow in knowledge. Strengthening your soul does not have to be mystical; simply getting to know God better through prayer and reading scripture can be ways to develop a healthy soul.

Externally, the "being" aspects of an Ideal Existence shift your attention to other people and resources. Healthy relationships are crucial for joy and peace. Of course, this includes your family, but should extend to friends and community too. Healthy finances might mean wealth, but it is much more about financial freedom (which can mean different things to different people). You get to define your relationship with money, and it is important to do so when devising your πDest. Finally, time is scarce and fleeting. How you use the time available to you AND minimizing your time being consumed by factors outside your control & desires are both important for an Ideal Existence.

Boiling it down a little, a πDest:

- Defines your future (healthy body, mind, soul, relationships, finances, and time)
- Is driven by purpose
- Sets direction and demands action
- Is a personal Lighthouse
- Is an image of your future
- Has a beginning and an ending
- Grows out of your πComp and πMap

Here are some questions you can ask to begin the voyage of discovering your πDest:

- What do I want?
- What do I do next for maximum impact?
- Where am I going? What is my next destination?
- What does my life look like in 5 to 10 years?
- What is my BHAG?
- What am I going to accomplish that is so big, if God isn't in it, I will fail?[7]

---

[7] This is derived from a quote by Jamie Buckingham: "Attempt something so big, that unless God intervenes, it's bound to fail."

In the πNautilus, πDest is blue because of clear skies, mountain vistas, etc. Blue represents clarity, tranquility, stability, harmony, unity, trust, truth, confidence, security, cleanliness, order, loyalty, sky, and water.

In order to communicate your Personal Ideal Destination, you should develop a Lighthouse Statement. This document will summarize your πDest. It is a beacon; it is clear and bright. And it should draw you toward your πDest. It should illuminate your πDest for others to see. The guide for your Lighthouse Statement is at the back of the book too. Here is my Lighthouse Statement:

Figure 3

By the end of 2025 I am thriving in faith, work, family, generosity, and leisure. My relationships with all of my kids have been restored and are only getting better. Meanwhile, my marriage is also growing healthier and more fulfilling. Outside of my immediate family, I have (personally) helped 100 people find a path to their Ideal Destination. My work is teeming with success. As a 5-times best-selling author, my consulting business has become very lucrative. I'm also flipping 5 houses every year. Despite giving 20% to church & charities and reinvesting profits into the business every year, my personal income has exceeded $250,000 per year for the first time ever. We live in our dream-home which has all the features & amenities we have wanted (large enough to entertain while small enough to maintain, in-ground pool with enclosure, pole barn, large kitchen with plenty of storage, laundry room near the master bedroom, beautiful woodwork & staircase, and an elevator.) In addition, we have a second home on the ocean in a warm climate. Both homes are near a small airport where we can fly on a small plane (I have my pilot's license now). We travel 5 weeks out of the year (3 weeks as a couple and 2 weeks for family vacations.) I still play volleyball weekly and work out, and I read 20 books per year.

When you think you are done, ask yourself if you can visualize it. Will anyone who reads it be able to visualize it? Does it have a beginning and an end? Do you know when you expect to arrive? Will you know when you get there?

Chapter 7: Personal Indicator Points

Speakers and life coaches everywhere talk about the importance of goals. And they are right. Goals are extremely important. Without the foundation of values, purpose, and destination (or Personal Integrity Compass, Personal Identity Map, and Personal Ideal Destination), goals are less effective than they should be. Without purpose and direction, goals can easily be misguided.

With that foundation in place, you can create goals that build on that foundation. A Personal Indicator Point (πPoint) is a specific objective that helps you move toward your πDest (an indicator of progress toward that destination). That is what a goal should be, but a πPoint has a specific formula for success. There are many references to SMART goals throughout goal and strategy literature. In order to be an effective tool, a πPoint must also encompass those concepts, but they, too, have been retooled with a new acronym. πPoints are **MILESTONES**:

Measurable
Integrated
Legitimate
Elevating
Simple
Temporal
Optimistic
Navigable
Encompassing

Specific

An effective πPoint must first be **Measurable** (as in quantity). This can be dollars, size, count, etc. So, a πPoint has to include a phrase like "double my contributions to 20%", "increase my community involvement by volunteering at 1 additional charity", or "increase my income to $100,000 per year". Those are quantifiable and therefore measurable.

So, what is meant by "**Integrated**"? Every πPoint must be fully aligned with your πComp, πMap, and πDest. This should not be assumed. Rather, it is imperative that each πPoint is tested against the Legend Statement (Cardinal Directives & πMap) and the Lighthouse Statement (πDest). Is it helping you reach your Personal Ideal Destination?

In terms of a πPoint, **Legitimate** refers to legality and ethics. To be a legitimate πPoint, it must be legal and ethical. Plain and simple.

πPoints should pull you in an upward direction. Just as importantly though, **Elevating** is about *significant*, upward progress. Each πPoint should be like a step on a staircase. Each step provides significant progress upward to the next floor. Have you ever walked up a set of stairs with unusually short steps? Not only does it feel awkward (almost like you are about to trip), but it feels like it takes forever to get to the top. That is what we want to avoid in properly written πPoints. A πPoint should stretch you; it should not be easy to achieve. You need πPoints that require some faith to achieve (either by their magnitude or short timeline).

The **Simpler** the πPoint the better it will be. Complex goals are difficult to achieve due to lack of focus and difficulty recognizing achievement. An effectively written (simple) πPoint is easy to work towards and easy to recognize when you get there.

Temporal has to do with time. All πPoints are time-bound meaning there is a date by which they are to be completed. This helps track progress toward the πPoint and the πDest. Are you on schedule? Behind? Ahead? And if so, by how much?

Similar to (but distinct from) "elevating", πPoints need to be **Optimistic**. The distinction is subtle, but Optimistic refers to polarity, or positive instead of negative. So, Optimistic πPoints promote positive growth or expansion (rather than negative action or retraction). For example, it is better to focus on "*increasing* effective use of downtime" rather than "*decreasing* amount of wasted time".

Of course, that optimism should be tempered/balanced by realism. So, every πPoint does need to be **Navigable** (achievable). Setting unattainable goals is disheartening and leads to abandoning the process and even the destination.

In addition, πPoints taken collectively should be **Encompassing**. In other words, have you covered all the bases? Are they at regular intervals towards the πDest (either in progress and/or time)? Are there πPoints for each "leg" of your iDest? Back to the Vacation Analogy… if you are driving from Indiana to Florida, and all your πPoints are in the initial four hours of the drive, progress for the remaining 16+ hours has no incremental achievements. Also, what about the πPoints leading up to the trip (like a savings amount to be reached, arranging a dog-sitter, etc.) Likewise, if your πPoints are all just cities, your kids will get pretty bored. There should be landmarks along the way. You should plan to stop at state parks or museums *en route*. Perhaps a certain restaurant or the hotel mid-trip can be a πPoint. Regardless, make sure that the entire voyage from your Big Red Dot (your starting point) to your πDest has Personal Indicator Points along the way. And every major step along the way should have a corresponding πPoint.

Finally, πPoints need to be **Specific**. This brings balance to over-simplification. πPoints need to be as Simple as possible, but too simple yields vagueness. In order to be clear (for accountability, for working to achieve them, and recognizing when they have been achieved), πPoints need specificity. Think in terms of the reporter's questions… who, what, when, where, and how much (we do not necessarily want the why in a πPoint, and "how much" is more useful here than simply "how").

By ensuring that your Indicator Points are truly MILESTONES, you will have clear way-markers on the voyage from your Big Red Dot to your Personal Ideal Destination. More importantly, you know the goals to accomplish, each of which will bring you closer to your πDest.

Figure 4

On the πNautilus, the πPoints section is orange. Orange is bold and unique (nothing rhymes with "orange"). Orange typically symbolizes energy, balance, expansiveness, and demanding of attention.

There is a recommended formula for phrasing πPoints. They are worded "as if now", meaning in the present tense. So, "It is now (future date) ... I am/have (fill in the blank)." In order to demonstrate the power of these characteristics, we will look first at an example of a well-worded πPoint then at a few missing some of these components.

Example of a good πPoint:

"It is now December 31, 2021 and I earned $50,000 in personal income for the year.

Ok, let's check... Is it Measurable? Yep ($50,000). Integrated? Yes. Legitimate? Absolutely. Elevating? For sure (it is a stretch goal since I started the year with a handful of clients in my new business). Simple? Yep. Temporal? Definitely. Optimistic? Yes. Navigable? It is. Encompassing? Well, not by itself. Specific? Check. Ok, so provided that my other πPoints Encompass all of the aspects of my πDest, we can say that this πPoint is valid.

So, what happens when elements are missing?

"It is now December 31, 2025 and I have 10 new clients…"

Wow, all I must do is book 2 clients per year for the next 5 years… and I will be out of business.

"By December 31, 2021 I have significantly increased my income."

Hmmm. How much is "significant"? Is 10% increase significant? How about doubling my income? That is a matter of opinion AND it depends on where I started (10% increase on $50,000 may not be significant, but 10% on $500,000 might be).

"On March 31, 2021 I have earned $150,000."

As I write this, it is the end of December 2020. In three months, am I really going to earn $150,000 having never built this kind of business before? While it is possible, it is beyond a stretch-goal… It is simply not Navigable.

Each of the MILESTONES components is important in every πPoint. Every single time.

Eric K. Beschinski

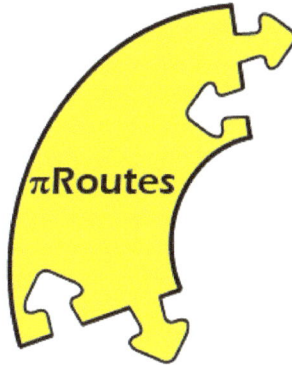

Chapter 8: Personal Incremental Routes

ersonal Incremental Routes (πRoutes) are the plans of collective smaller steps necessary to accomplish each πPoint. They are action plans or project management. Each πRoute contains a series of action items that when completed yield a successful πPoint.

Obviously, since there are many Personal Indicator Points on the way to your Personal Ideal Destination, there need to be πRoutes for each of these πPoints. These are the requirements to arrive at each πPoint, and they become tasks (in the next chapter). You are the Helmsman for your voyage, so you are responsible for each πRoute. In order to be effective, each πRoute needs to show how the parts tie together and the timeline for completion of each part.

πRoutes are the routes that get you from your Big Red Dot to your 1st πPoint (or from πPoint to πPoint). And let's face it, the Vacation Analogy only goes so far. Getting to your πDest is not nearly as linear as a family vacation. So, your πPoints (if they are Encompassing) may not be linear. There may be multiple projects working simultaneously toward distinct πPoints that are functionally unrelated. That is all normal.

As for timelines, sometimes it is useful to think in terms of halfway markers. In addition to thinking through all the action steps, ask what it will look like when you are halfway to the πPoint. Note that marker. What will it look like when you are halfway to that marker? Repeat until you have a manageable piece of work to identify on your πRoute.

This is also where you want to start factoring in costs. Naturally, financial costs are part of the equation, but you also want to consider relationships, time, productivity (diverted work or learning curve), and emotional costs.

πRoutes are yellow in the πNautilus, and yellow frequently represents joy, happiness, optimism, idealism, imagination, hope, and gold.

To help organize and visualize πRoutes, the πNautilus Radar was developed. This tool will help you break your πDest into "currents" or components. When you plot your πPoints on each current, you can more easily see where there are gaps (so you can ensure your πPoints are Encompassing). In addition, the spaces between each πPoint on each current becomes a πRoute. There are instructions and an example in

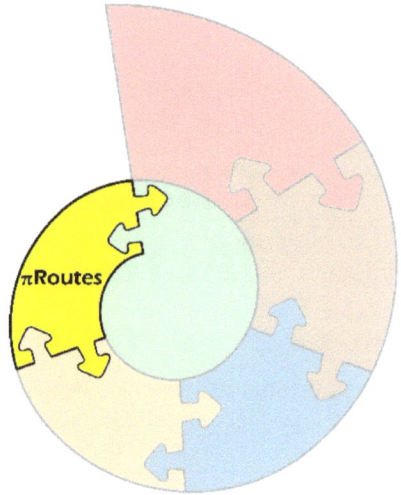

Figure 5

Appendix C (and the πNautilus Radar™ can be downloaded for free at http://www.piNautilus.com).

Chapter 9: Personal Immediate Tasks

The logical center of the πNautilus consists of Personal Immediate Tasks (πTasks). These are defined as the daily actions on which to focus your time and energy. Obviously, this can be a large list of activities. There are several purposes for πTasks that need to be factored.

First, there is the progressive step from Personal Incremental Routes to execution of the Personal Immediate Tasks on each πRoute. This is where the rubber meets the road. Each Personal Immediate Task accomplished brings each πRoute to fruition. In turn, making it to the end of each πRoute culminates at the corresponding πPoint. Once all the πPoints have been reached, the πDest is near.

This is where execution becomes the central focus. As you shift out of planning mode and into action, πTasks become the center of attention (they are also the center of the πNautilus). While this shift is crucial, it is also important to avoid tunnel vision. Your entire πNautilus needs to be firmly planted in your mind so that the πTasks bridge to all your plans. This will come together more cohesively in the next chapter.

Then there is the internal-analysis purpose of πTasks… Beyond the scope of the path to a πDest, πTasks provide a means of course correction. As you are navigating through this process, it is vital to ensure you remain on course. You should regularly be asking the following questions about your activity:

1. Does this πTask align with the πComp and πMap?
2. Does this πTask actually help me reach my πDest?

As for the first question, this had better be a "yes." If something you are doing violates your values or purpose, make it stop or fix it. Immediately.

Regarding the second question about πTasks, if the answer is "yes", then you can consider it a **Tailwind πTask**. It is propelling you forward along your voyage to your πDest. Effort and resources should be maximized to ensure that this πTask can get accomplished on time or ahead of schedule.

If the answer to that 2nd question is "no", some follow up is necessary. Obviously, there are day-to-day activities that do not directly move you toward a πDest, but they are essential, nonetheless. Bill paying, for example, might fall into this category. You cannot eliminate time spent paying bills. These types of activities would be **Crosswind πTasks**. If you are not mindful, they could potentially blow you off course. Monitor them closely and ensure that only the resources/time absolutely necessary are devoted to Crosswind πTasks.

Then there are **Headwind πTasks**. These are the πTasks that are working against your progress to the πDest. They could be something directly opposed to the strategy. For example, if the πDest involves shifting from a factory job to a full-time author, taking 2 years of welding classes to further that career might be a Headwind πTask. More often, however, a Headwind πTask will come in the form of a non-essential activity that is diverting resources from Tailwind πTasks. So, maybe your factory job provides you considerable time off. Taking a second job in your off time so you have extra money for a boat is example of a Headwind πTask.

Headwind πTasks should be eliminated. This can be difficult since it may require sacrificing things you enjoy and/or telling people "no". Nobody said that reaching a Personal Ideal Destination was going to be easy or painless. It will be worth it though. Remember that every action you agree to do, every time you say "yes" to a request for resources (be it money, time, etc.), you are saying "no" to everything else that could be using those resources. Let me say that again. Every "yes" to one thing, is a "no" to everything else. Tim Hartford said it best, "Every time we say yes to a request, we are also saying no to anything else we might accomplish with the time." [8]

---

[8] "The Power of Saying No" by Tim Hartford, <u>Financial Times</u>, Copyright © 2015

This is true for your own life and for any organization you might lead. Value your time.

This means that you will have to say "no" to things that are very good, maybe even excellent. That's OK. There are an infinite number of ways to spend your time, and very many of them are "good". And despite an abundance mentality, time is one of the only truly scarce resources. No matter what you do (unlike money, ideas, friends, etc.) you can never make more of it. It is important to align the use of your time with your values, purpose, and destination. Say "yes" to good things only if they are aligned with your πDest.

To illustrate, suppose you were asked to sit on a board for a local non-profit organization. Agreeing to sitting on a board that will only require one night per month is still a rejection of EVERY OTHER possible use for that night. Every month. (I am by no means suggesting that sitting on a board is a bad thing. I am simply saying that there are only 31 evenings in a month. Be mindful about how you are spending them.)

Along with creating clear plans and action items, it is also important to define clear objectives for everyone involved in your plan. Since it is highly unlikely (and definitely not advisable) that you will do this alone, it is vitally important to set proper expectations for the friends, family, colleagues, and delegees in your πNautilus. Most human conflict arises from unmet expectations. That can be the result of people not doing what they are supposed to do. However, it is also common that accurate expectations were never defined or communicated in the first place.

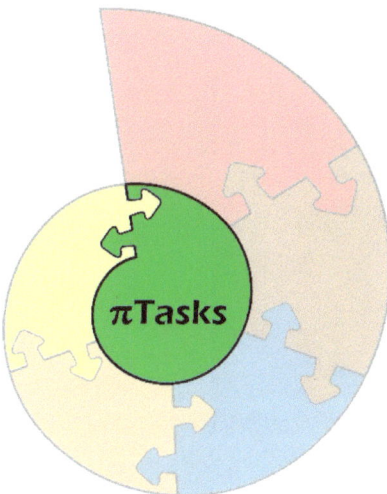

Figure 7

Now that you are working through the process of planning your πDest, take the time to clearly define the roles and actions you will need from your "team" to be successful. When you do this, keep πTasks at the forefront. Define objectives based on the πTasks and πRoutes.

On the πNautilus, πTasks are green, because green is the color of nature, the environment, healthiness, good luck, renewal, fertility, service, and vigor. Hence, action and life.

Eric K. Beschinski

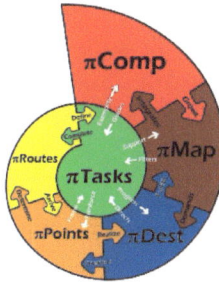

Chapter 10: The Personal Integrated Nautilus (πNautilus™)

T his is where things start getting fun(er) and concepts begin to intertwine. Connections are made. Light bulbs go on. So far, we have identified the 6 major components of the πNautilus, and those are (in order) πComp, πMap, πDest, πPoints, πRoutes, and πTasks. These are the Ports of your voyage. Each requires you to stop, strategize, reload, and depart again.

As you can see on the complete πNautilus (Figure 8 on page 39, and you will probably want to hold your finger there so you can flip back and forth between Figure 8 and the text of this chapter), there are links between each of the Ports. These are called Bridges and Anchors. Furthermore, each link has an arrow indicating a direction.

Bridges

The inward bridges flow from the start (the πComp) of the πNautilus clockwise towards the center (πTasks). This follows the natural progression through the process of strategy + execution that the πNautilus is designed to demonstrate. It also provides a "star chart" for Navigating the decision-making process, helping to ensure that every decision is made without sidetracking you from your purpose and destination.

The first bridge is noted by the word "Grow". Very simply, your πMap should Grow from your πComp. It is an organic process.

With Cardinal Directives as seeds, leaders cultivate that πMap. One cannot expect an apple tree from an acorn, nor can one raise an oak and say it came from watermelon seeds. That is the nature of the relationship between Cardinal Directives and Purpose. All said and done, any right-minded individual should be able to read your πComp, then see the πMap and say, "Well, that makes sense." The same individual should also be able to see the πMap then the πComp and say, "Of course."

As the voyage continues, the next bridge is represented by the word "Demands," because a clear πMap will Demand a πDest (next big destination) in order to move continually toward fulfillment. Once again, the adjacent Ports of the πNautilus are distinct but closely related.

Discernment is needed to begin the process of breaking the πDest voyage into logical πPoints. The bridge linking πDest to πPoints is designated by "Charters." A Personal Ideal Destination Charters the Personal Indicator Points. πDest (as the Lighthouse for direction and "final" destination) is the driving force that determines what πPoints are appropriate for you.

From πPoints the next logical step is to deduce the Personal Incremental Routes. Quite simply, an action plan is the series of events necessary to complete a goal on time and on target. It is for this reason that πPoints "Determine" the πRoutes.

The next bridge is a crucial step. πRoutes "Define" Personal Immediate Tasks, meaning that πRoute steps are taken one at a time and converted into the daily activity which is where the real work gets done. πTasks must be managed daily in order to make continual progress forward. This activity includes review of the prior steps, completion of items in the πRoutes (or progress on them), and reflecting on the Personal Integrity Compass, Personal Identity Map, and Personal Ideal Destination.

The outward bridges flow from the center of the πNautilus counterclockwise back to πComp. Just as each section of the πNautilus leads ever inward toward πTasks, those πTasks in turn drive outward back through the πNautilus.

πTasks should lead toward completion of the πRoutes. Each day, as you conduct business, every action should be evaluated to ensure that it is helping "Complete" steps on the πRoutes. (There may be some πTasks that are necessary but have no corresponding πRoutes steps. As mentioned in Chapter 9, these Crosswind πTasks should be evaluated to ensure that they are either fully aligned or truly necessary).

As steps from πRoutes are achieved, the bridge to πPoints is crossed as you move towards each πPoint. In other words, Personal Incremental Routes allow you to "Arrive" at the Personal Indicator Points.

When each πPoint is achieved it helps to "Realize" the Personal Ideal Destination. This is perhaps the most important part of the methodology… it is the crux of why you are doing all of this work in your life. You want to realize a vision, or in this case your Personal Ideal Destination.

Fully Realizing the current πDest helps "Fulfill" the Personal Identity Map. Remember, your πMap is equivalent to your purpose. When you reach your Personal Ideal Destination, you should have made significant movement toward fulfilling that purpose.

While a πMap is never completely fulfilled, a true πMap will always support the πComp and "Integrate" those Cardinal Directives throughout your life.

Anchors

Finally, the real magic behind the πNautilus is about to reveal itself. Although it has already been a natural progression, the reason for the πNautilus shape hinges around πTasks. The πNautilus is the only 2-dimensional shape that demonstrates progression inward AND outward in a spiral while also allowing the center (πTasks) to touch each stage or Port. So, as already mentioned, moving inward the Personal Integrity Compass **grows** the Personal Identity Map which **demands** a Personal Ideal Destination in order to **charter** Personal Indicator Points. Then the πPoints **determine** Personal Incremental Routes which **define** Personal Immediate Tasks. In reverse, πTasks **complete** πRoutes which **arrive** at πPoints in order to **realize** the πDest, helping to **fulfill** the πMap. And finally, the πMap **integrates** with the πComp.

Anchors provide the final connections. Each anchor links the πTasks with every other Port of the πNautilus. So, πTasks should always **Reinforce** the πPoints, and πPoints should **Frame** your πTasks. Likewise, πTasks should always **Progress** the πDest, and the πDest should **Direct** every πTask. All πTasks should **Support** the πMap, and the πMap should **Filter** all πTasks. Finally, all of your πTasks should **Exemplify** the πComp (Cardinal Directives), and the πComp should **Guide** those πTasks.

This framework pushes you to check every decision (major and minor) to ensure it is moving you toward your vision while supporting your purpose and aligning with your core values. Therein lies the power of the Personal Integrated Nautilus (piNautilus or πNautilus).

Personal Integrated Nautilus (πNautilus™)

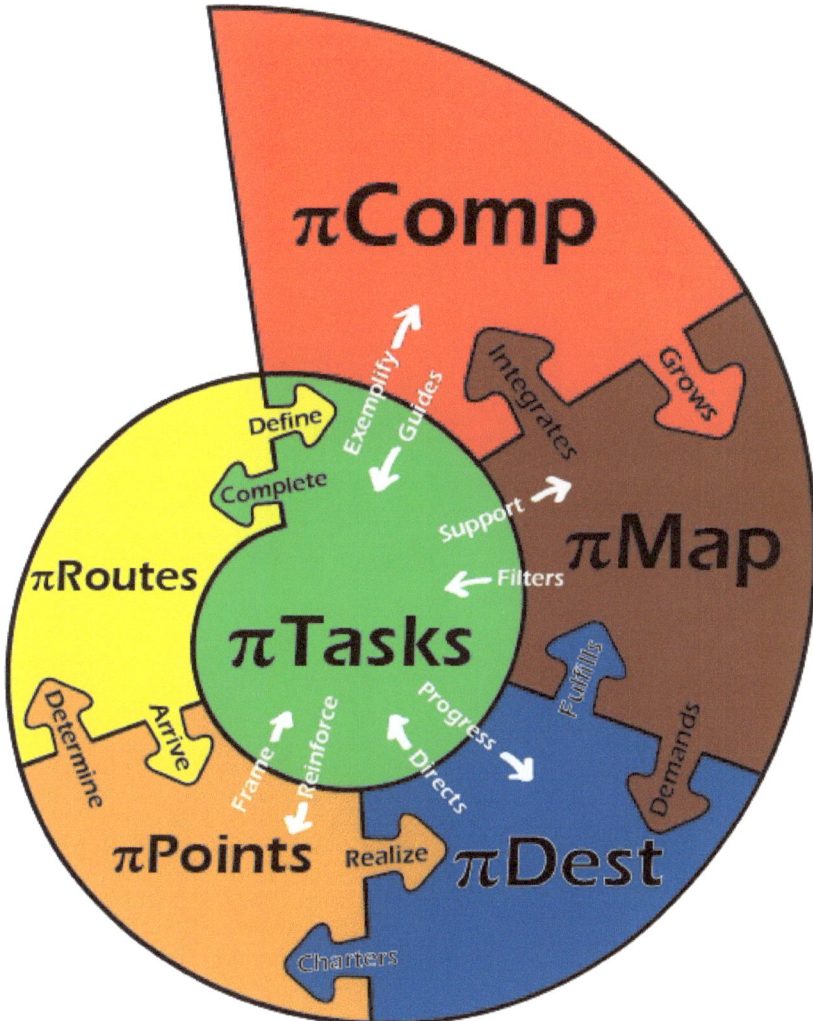

Figure 8

Eric K. Beschinski

Chapter 11: Arrival! (or not)

Keep in mind that this is a Plan. Plans are subject to change. Back to our Vacation. What happens when you run into a detour (maybe you cannot find a publisher willing to take a risk on you or you are downsized from your job before you were ready to go full-time with your new direction.) This is to be expected. When you expect the unexpected (even in vague terms) you strip that event of the power to derail you. Do not scrap the entire plan. Instead, adapt. Maybe there is a new πPoint to consider (with a new πRoute and πTasks). You go back to the drawing board and revise the plan.

So, you are moving along toward your πDest, checking πTasks off your πRoutes. Then something unthinkable happens. Your Personal Ideal Destination is no longer ideal. Maybe the business landscape has changed. Maybe your heart has changed. Maybe God has called you in a different direction. That's OK too. Reorient. Start from where you are in that moment and identify your new Big Red Dot. Check in on your πComp and πMap and start selecting a new πDest.

These are more than course corrections; they are full-on changes of direction. Do not be (overly) alarmed. It is not that unusual, and it does not necessarily need to be perceived as a negative. After all, you have no way to really know what it will be like to be in the πDest until you are actually there. Maybe the closer you get, the more you realize that it is not what you were hoping. You now have a better perspective and can choose a new πDest with more experience behind the decision.

Some people love the journey. I am a destination person. For me, the journey was usually just a means to an end. I discovered that was a severely limited perspective. Many things can be enjoyed on the journey. There is beauty to be seen. There are experiences to be had. And there is continual growth. If you never reach a πDest, that is not failure. Maybe your πDest keeps changing. Maybe no matter how hard you work at it, you simply never arrive. Keep checking that you are on the right course and keep evaluating that your πDest is still your Personal Ideal Destination. And keep moving forward. If you get stuck, do not stay stuck. God never promises that he will fulfill all our plans or that we will succeed in all our endeavors. So, actively enjoy the journey every day.

Otherwise, if you do not run into those kinds of issues, execute, Execute, EXECUTE. Make your πDest your new reality.

Then you reach your πDest. Now what? Well, first of all, pause. Enjoy the arrival and the destination you worked so hard to make a reality. Have that drink on the beach with a good book.

Also, take time to acknowledge the accomplishment. Show gratitude to those who contributed. Look around you to soak in the beauty of your new surroundings for a moment. Think back to your Big Red Dot and note the changes in your life and yourself. Reflect upon and learn from the mistakes along the way. This is the only time (brief though it should be) that it is alright not to have a πDest. But do not rest too long in the revelry.

Once you hit un-pause and the "Vacation" is over, it is time to start anew. You have a new Big Red Dot. Check in on your πComp and πMap and start choosing a new πDest. As previously quoted from T.S. Elliot, and so coming back to where we started: "...To make an end is to make a beginning."

If you found value in this book, please leave a review on Amazon at http://Amazon.piNautilus.com, and thank you for reading my book! Also, additional information and resources are available in the following pages and appendices.

Appendix A: Bridges

Each Bridge has a name. Since it does not really matter if you never remember the names of the Bridges as long as you understand the concepts, I summarized the concepts in Chapter 10 and included the details here.

Life Bridges

The first Bridges (arrows linking Ports on the πNautilus) are the Life Bridges, because the πComp, πMap, and the links between them define the very nature of your existence, your life. The **Inward Life Bridge** is the name of the directional link from πComp to πMap. In the πNautilus, this bridge is noted by the word "Grow". A person's πMap should Grow organically from his or her πComp.

Although a πMap is never completely fulfilled, an accurate πMap will always support the πComp and "Integrate" those Cardinal Directives throughout one's life. That is the **Outward Life Bridge**.

Directional Bridges

The Directional Bridges are the links between the πMap and the πDest. The **Inward Directional Bridge** is so named since the direction of your life should always be defined by the πMap and πDest, and it is represented by the word "Demands." The πMap should Demand a πDest (next big destination) in order to move continually toward fulfillment.

As for the **Outward Directional Bridge**, this link between Ports deals with the relationship from πDest back to πMap. Again, Realizing (making a reality) the πDest helps "Fulfill" the Personal Identity Map.

Discerning Bridges

Discernment is needed break the πDest voyage into logical πPoints and to realize when the πDest has been achieved. Therefore, the Discerning Bridges link πDest and πPoints. The **Inward Discerning Bridge** is the inward-bound arrow designated by "Charters."

The **Outward Discerning Bridge** is crossed when each πPoint helps "Realize" the Personal Ideal Destination.

Deductive Bridges

Since deductive reasoning is significant for the link between πPoints and πRoutes, these are the Deductive Bridges. On the **Inward Deductive Bridge**, πPoints "Determine" the πRoutes while on the **Outward Deductive Bridge**, πRoutes help you "Arrive" at each πPoint.

Incremental Bridges

Goals are achieved by taking one step at a time. This incrementalism is why the links between πRoutes and πTasks are the Incremental Bridges. Specifically, πRoutes "Define" πTasks on the **Inward Incremental Bridge**. Meanwhile, getting πTasks done helps to "Complete" each πRoute (**Outward Incremental Bridge**).

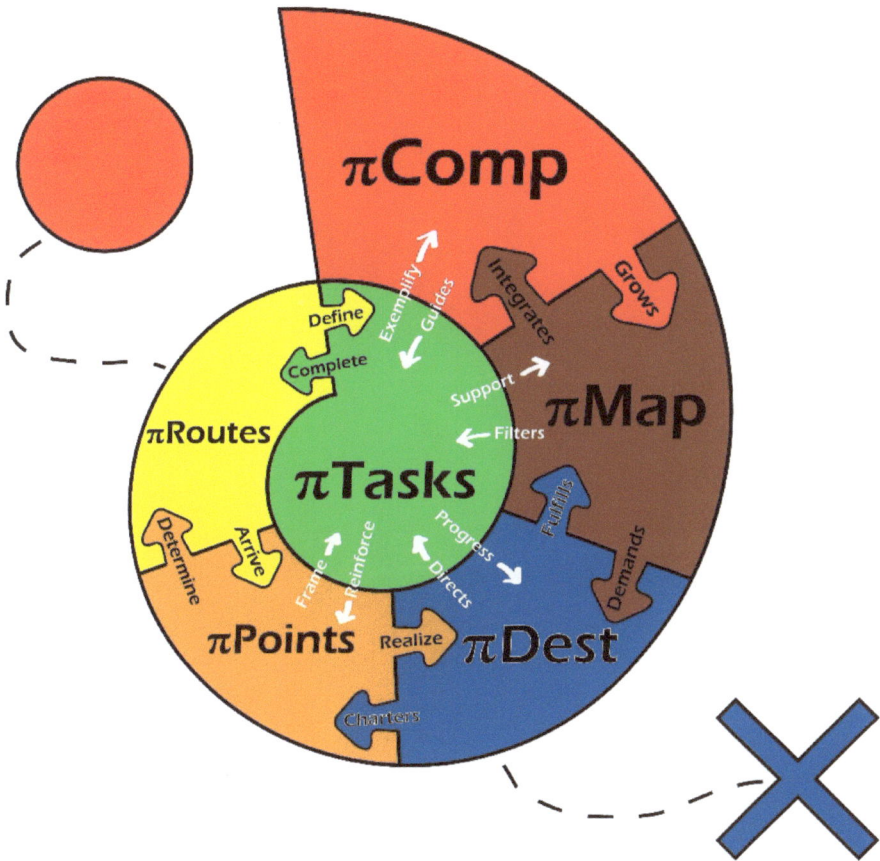

Eric K. Beschinski

Appendix B: Resources

The following resources are provided in the subsequent pages (you will probably need to make copies of some of them OR you can download PDF 8.5x11" versions at www.piNautilus.com):

- Big Red Dot template
- πComp Worksheet
- Cardinal Directives Worksheet
- Legend Statement template
- Lighthouse Statement template
- πNautilus Radar™ (see Appendix C for details)
- πPoints Worksheet
- πRoute Builder
- πTasks Worksheet
- Vector Modeling™ Daily Worksheet (see Appendix D for details)

In addition, Greenfire Innovations is available for coaching and live programs:

- A variety of coaching and training programs are detailed at www.GreenfireInnovations.com.
- The author is available for speaking engagements related to the πNautilus and iNautilus methodologies.

- For any of these coaching and speaking opportunities plus other resources, please see the πNautilus Network at www.piNautilus.com.

Big Red Dot™

What am I doing with my life right now? (NOT WHY, just WHAT)

What is my current reach?

Whom do I influence?

What are my stats? (age, income, family size, etc...)

What words define me?

What contribution/impact am I making on the world or my community right now?

Who am I? Who would others say I am? Who would God say I am?

What do I believe about myself? What is the truth about those beliefs?

Where am I right now (current status, standing, and situation)?

Big Red Dot™

πComp™ Worksheet
Personal Integrity Compass™
Write 4 to 8 Cardinal Directives™

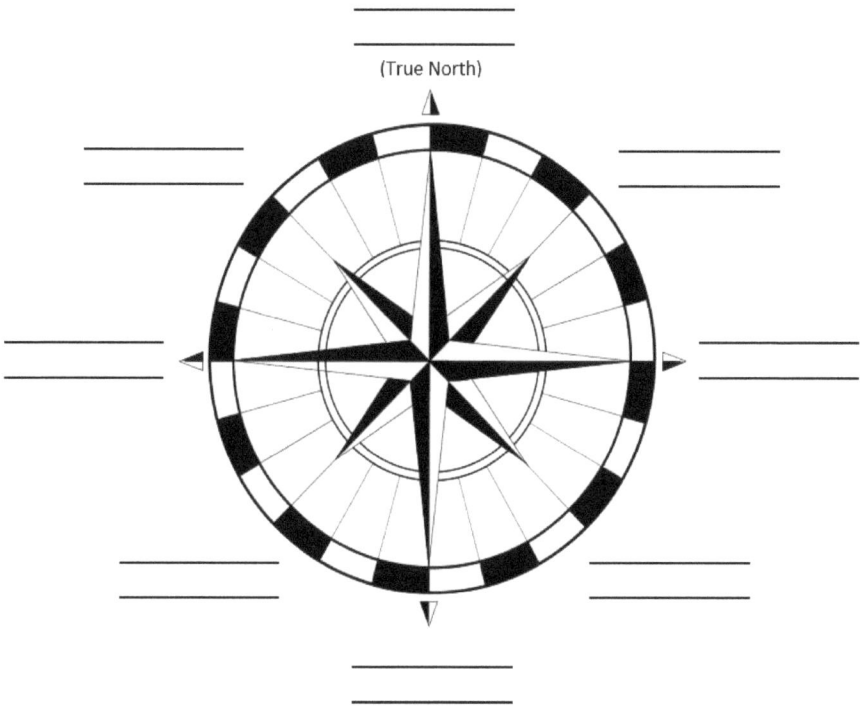

_____
_____
(True North)

_____   _____

_____   _____

_____
_____

Eric K. Beschinski

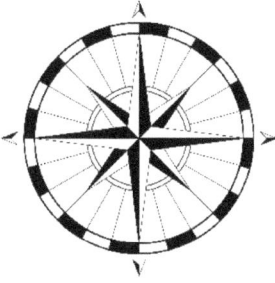

Cardinal Directives™
Worksheet

True North: _____ _____

Description: _____

_____

East (right): _____ _____

Description: _____

_____

South (bottom): _____ _____

Description: _____

_____

West (left): _____ _____

Description: _____

_____

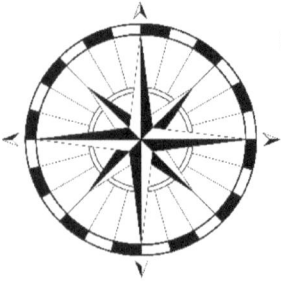

Cardinal Directives™ Worksheet

NorthEast: _____ _____

Description: _____

_____

SouthEast: _____ _____

Description: _____

_____

SouthWest: _____ _____

Description: _____

_____

NorthWest: _____ _____

Description: _____

_____

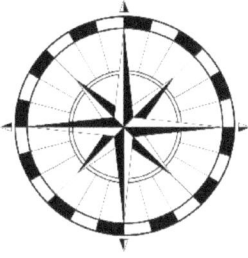

Legend Statement™

What do I value most? What is my True North?

Why do I exist?

What is my calling?

Why am I in this geographic location?

What am I designed to do?

What am I passionate about?

What makes me exceedingly joyful?

What angers my sensibilities?

Where am I right now (current status, standing, and situation)?

Legend Statement™

_____

_____

_____

_____

_____

_____

_____

_____

_____

_____

_____

_____

Legend Statement™

_____

_____

_____

_____

_____

_____

_____

_____

_____

_____

_____

_____

_____

_____

_____

_____

Legend Statement™

_____

_____

_____

_____

_____

_____

_____

_____

_____

_____

_____

_____

_____

_____

Lighthouse
Statement™

What do I want?

What do I do next as the ideal version of myself?

Where am I going? What is my destination?

What does my life look like in 5 to 10 years?

What is my BHAG?

What am I going to accomplish that is so big I can hardly imagine it?

What words do I want to define me?

Who do I want to be? Who does God want me to be?

What contribution/impact on the world do I want to be my legacy?

Start with a lead-in sentence (summary, easy to remember, symbolic of the whole πDest).

Lighthouse Statement™

Lighthouse Statement™

Lighthouse Statement™

Can you visualize your πDest?

Will anyone who reads it be able to visualize it?

Does it have a beginning and an end?

Do you know when you expect to arrive?

Will you know when you get there?

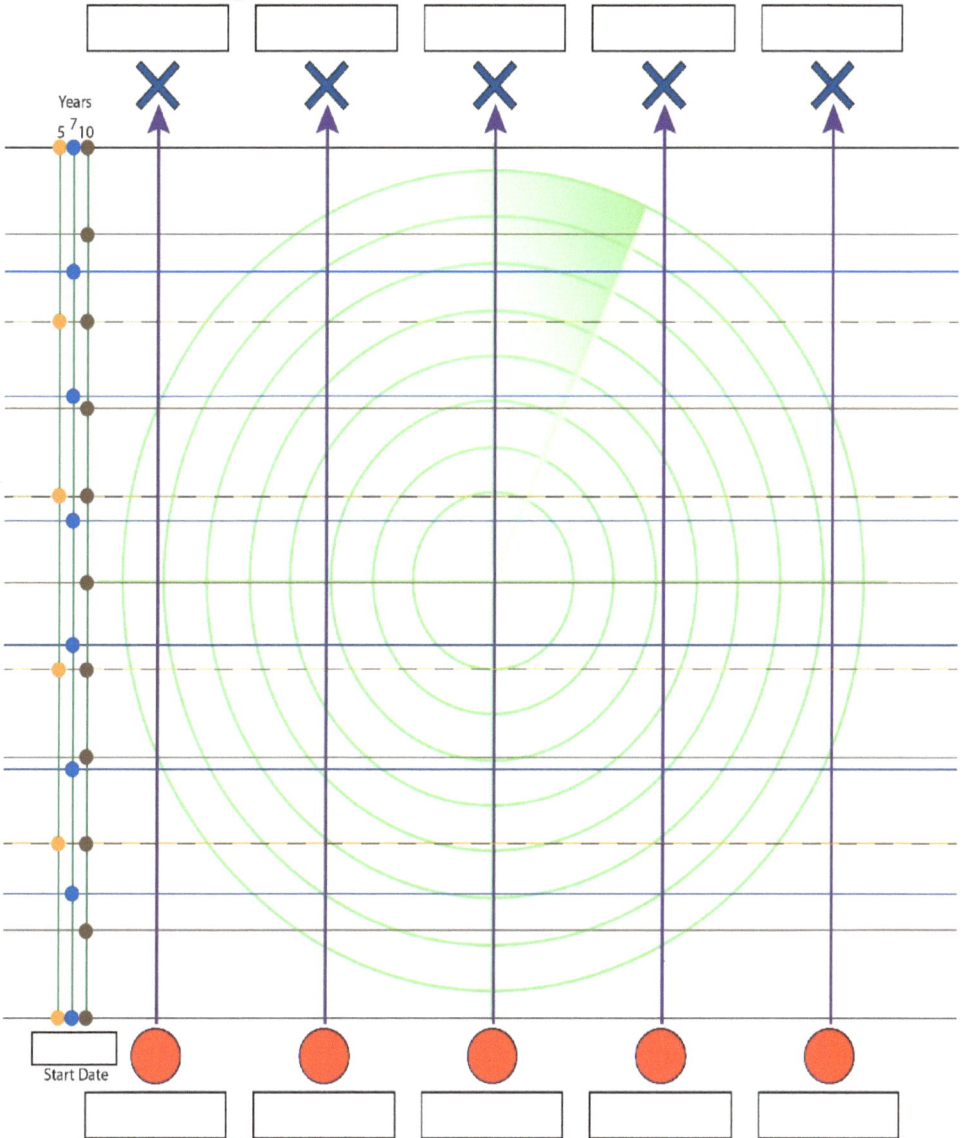

An 8½ x 11 PDF version of the πNautilus Radar is available at www.piNautilus.com, and instructions are in Appendix C.

Eric K. Beschinski

πPoints™

Measurable Integrated Legitimate Elevating Simple Temporal Optimistic Navigable Encompassing Specific

It is now _____, □ □ □ □ □ □ □ □ □ □

and I am/have

_____

_____.

It is now _____, □ □ □ □ □ □ □ □ □ □

and I am/have

_____

_____.

It is now _____, □ □ □ □ □ □ □ □ □ □

and I am/have

_____

_____.

It is now _____, □ □ □ □ □ □ □ □ □ □

and I am/have

_____

_____.

πPoints™

Measurable Integrated Legitimate Elevating Simple Temporal Optimistic Navigable Encompassing Specific

It is now _____, ☐ ☐ ☐ ☐ ☐ ☐ ☐ ☐ ☐ ☐

and I am/have

_____

_____.

It is now _____, ☐ ☐ ☐ ☐ ☐ ☐ ☐ ☐ ☐ ☐

and I am/have

_____

_____.

It is now _____, ☐ ☐ ☐ ☐ ☐ ☐ ☐ ☐ ☐ ☐

and I am/have

_____

_____.

It is now _____, ☐ ☐ ☐ ☐ ☐ ☐ ☐ ☐ ☐ ☐

and I am/have

_____

_____.

πRoute™ Builder

Which πPoint™ is this for?

_____
_____
_____

Project/Portion/Description:

_____
_____
_____

Who is the Helmsman?

_____
_____

Start Date: _____ Completion Date: _____

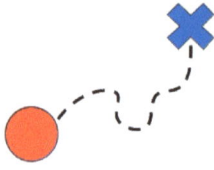

πRoute™ Builder

List of πTasks™

	πTask™	Who?	Due?
☐	_____	_____	_____
☐	_____	_____	_____
☐	_____	_____	_____
☐	_____	_____	_____
☐	_____	_____	_____
☐	_____	_____	_____
☐	_____	_____	_____
☐	_____	_____	_____
☐	_____	_____	_____
☐	_____	_____	_____
☐	_____	_____	_____
☐	_____	_____	_____
☐	_____	_____	_____
☐	_____	_____	_____
☐	_____	_____	_____

✔ πTask™ Worksheet

Describe the πTask™   Propeller? ☐

_____

_____

Which πRoute™ is this for?

_____

_____

Who "owns" this πTask™?

_____

_____

☐Tailwind   ☐Crosswind   or   ☐Headwind

Subsequent Action:

_____

_____

Start Date: _____ Completion Date: _____

Eric K. Beschinski

✓πTask™ Worksheet

Describe the πTask™   Propeller? ☐

_____

_____

Which πRoute™ is this for?

_____

_____

Who "owns" this πTask™?

_____

_____

☐Tailwind   ☐Crosswind   or   ☐Headwind
Subsequent Action:

_____

_____

Start Date: _____ Completion Date: _____

πNautilus™ Vector Modeling™ Daily Worksheet

Focal πRoute:

Crosswinds

Headwinds

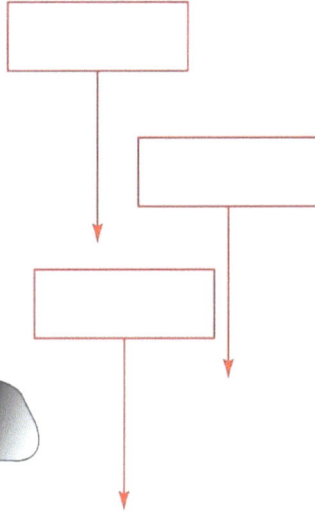

Propeller:

(Key πTask for Today)

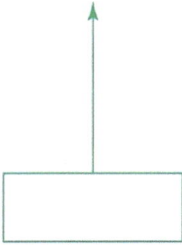

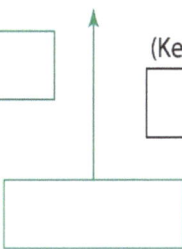

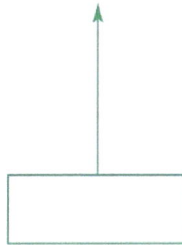

Tailwinds

An 8½ x 11 PDF version of the πNautilus Vector Modeling Daily Worksheet is available at www.piNautilus.com, and instructions are in Appendix D.

Eric K. Beschinski

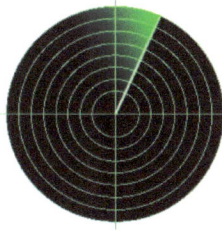

Appendix C: πNautilus Radar™

A birds-eye view of a plan is important. The πNautilus Radar is designed to provide such a view. Essentially, the Radar divides your πDest into segments, then allows you to plot your πPoints for each.

πNautilus Radar Instructions

Overview: The πNautilus Radar allows you to plot your πPoints on a visual "map" so you can track and plan your progress toward your πDest.

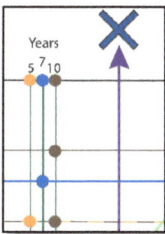

Each vertical arrow (purple) is a "current" and represents your progress for a component of your πDest. Below are detailed instructions and excerpts from the example Radar shown on the next page. The timeline on the left of the page is a guide to help you position your πPoints based on anticipated arrival dates. Enter today's date at the bottom then use the colored dots/lines based on the timeframe of your πDest (either 5, 7, or 10 years). See snapshot to the left.

1. First, you need to identify the various components of your πDest. Usually, there will be several, distinct aspects of your πDest than can be easily summarized in few words. Write these in the boxes above the "X's".

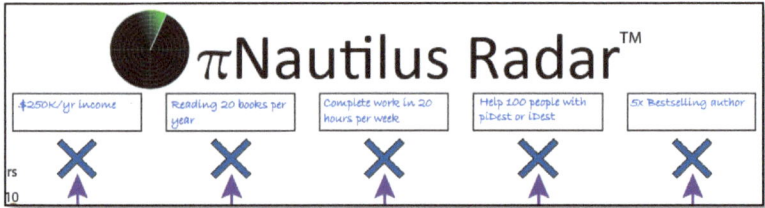

2. Identify where you are now (Big Red Dot) for each of these currents, and enter them below the corresponding red dot.

3. Now it's time to determine your πPoints for each of the currents. Start at the top (closest to your πDest X's, and draw a hollow circle

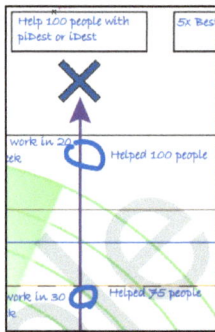

on the current and write a description of the πPoint next to it. Work your way down, asking yourself what is the preceding πPoint necessary to achieve each one. If you get stuck, start from the red dot and work your way up. Keep in mind that this is a fluid plan… you will probably need to make adjustments as you Navigate through it. Also, use the Radar to help ensure that your πPoints are "Encompassing"… covering all of the bases and distributed relatively evenly throughout the timeframe of your voyage. Look for large gaps between πPoints. Ask yourself if there is an intermediary step that should be an πPoint.

4. As you progress toward your πDest, use the Radar as a tool to track πPoint completion. Check each one off (or fill in the circle),

preferably with red, to indicate that you have arrived at that πPoint and it's time to look to the next.

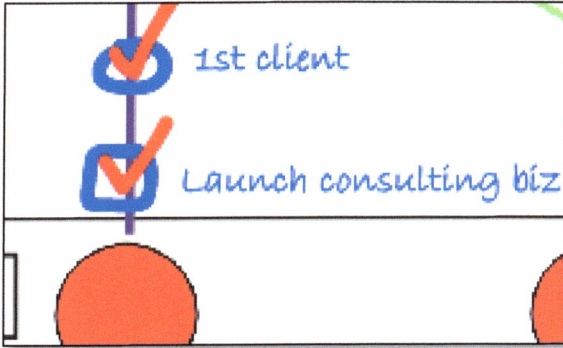

5.   Be sure to detail each πPoint on the πPoints Worksheets.

6.   Finally, the spaces between πPoints on a current are your πRoutes. Do not try to build πRoutes for all your πPoints at the beginning. Instead, build πRoutes from your Big Red Dot to the first πPoint on each current. When you reach an πPoint, build the πRoute to the next πPoint on that current. This process is designed to be linear so that you can track progress, have clarity, and focus on what is important.

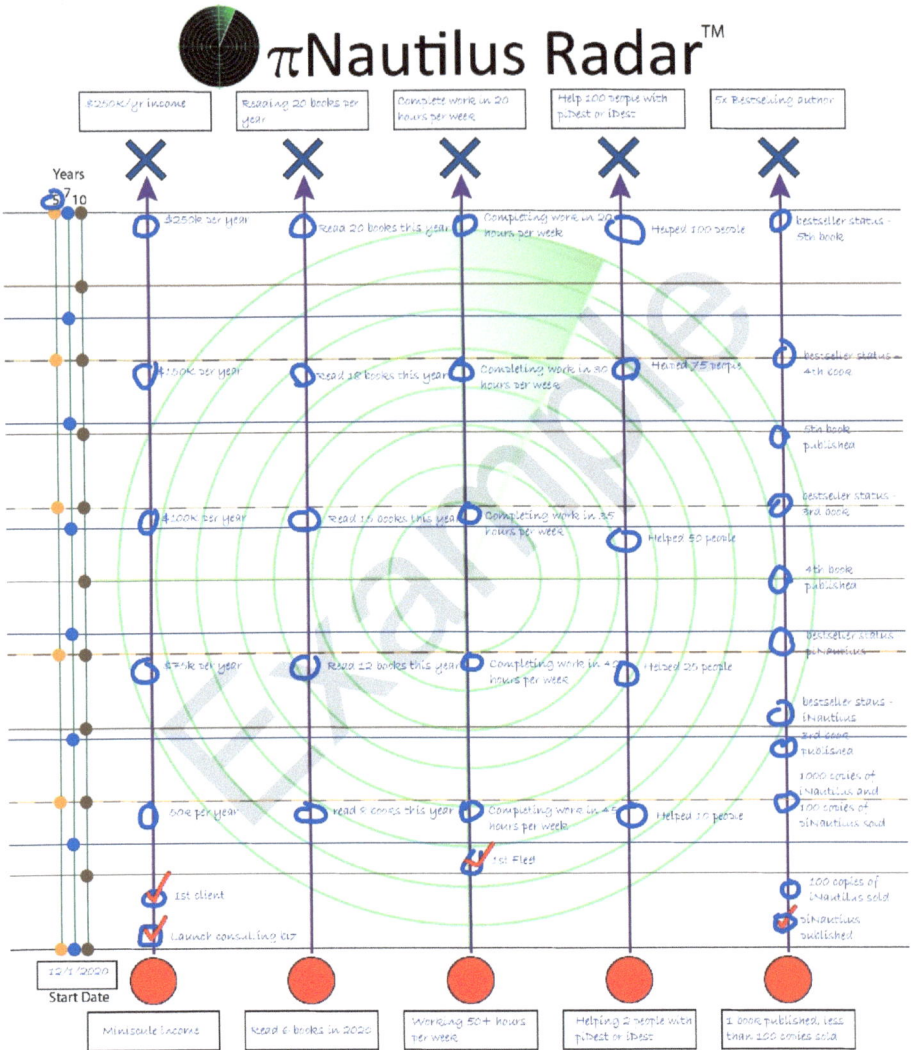

The πNautilus Radar worksheet is in the previous section with the other worksheets. However, I recommend downloading the 8½ x 11 PDF version from www.piNautilus.com

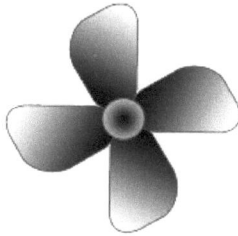

Appendix D: Propellers & Vector Modeling™

In order to make continual progress toward your πDest, it's imperative to plan daily activity. That's where Vector Modeling comes in. Simply put, Vector Modeling is the process of determining the day's most important πTask and anticipating distractions and obstacles ahead of time.

This "most important πTask" is called a Propeller since it is propelling you toward a πPoint. These are significant or important action items that will usually require longer periods of time to complete. If you do not plan for these and schedule time for them, then the day-to-day "smaller" πTasks will usually take precedence and cause you to procrastinate on the more important ones. Put time on your calendar for your Propellers, and work on them first.

In math and physics, a vector is direction + magnitude. So, in Vector Modeling you are ensuring that your activity is in the proper direction (a Propeller πTask leading ultimately toward the πDest), and then assigning a magnitude (number of hours you will devote to that Propeller πTask). In addition, you will write down any Crosswinds (distractions) and Headwinds (obstacles) you can think of that will get in the way of devoting your committed time to the Propeller πTask. Furthermore, you will identify any Tailwinds which are solutions or advocates that will help you complete your Propeller πTask.

πNautilus Vector Modeling Instructions

Overview: The πNautilus Vector Modeling provides a daily tool to help focus time and energy while also anticipating obstacles/distractions.

You will use at least 1 Vector Modeling worksheet per day with the intent of spending a minimum of 2 hours on activity that will help you reach your Personal Ideal Destination. πTasks that are key/important for achieving πPoints are called Propellers (these are "Big Rocks"). Each day you will select at least 1 Propeller πTask and dedicate time to its completion. Here's how to use the worksheet:

1. First, identify (using your completed Radar) which πRoute and subsequent Propeller πTask will be the focus for the day. These will be written on the Vector Modeling worksheet.

Daily Worksheet

Focal πRoute:

Help 1 person with piDest

Propeller:
(Key πTask for Today)

Schedule 5 coffee meetings

2. In the empty circle on the Vector arrowhead, enter the number of hours you will devote to this πTask for the day. A minimum of 2 hours is recommended, but you should commit to as much time as you can. Remember these are the Personal Immediate Tasks that are necessary to move forward through each πRoute to each πPoint in order to reach your πDest.

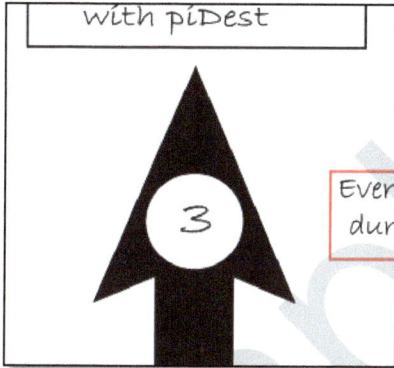

3. Block this time off in your calendar, preferably the first timeslot in the day. This time is "sacred". Turn off your phone. Close your browser windows and email programs. Prepare to focus on this πTask alone for the time you have designated.

4. Next, you will want to identify Crosswinds. These are anticipated distractions. These may be the same each day or they may vary. The point is to think through the possible distractions so that you recognize them and can respond appropriately. It is OK if these are unknown (or you run into one that you didn't anticipate.) Even writing "Unknown" in one of the lines is fine. Preparation will do several things for you including a) getting your mindset "on guard" for distractions, b) allowing you to more easily recognize them when they occur, c) setting you up to respond more quickly/easily to them, and d) removing power from these distractions.

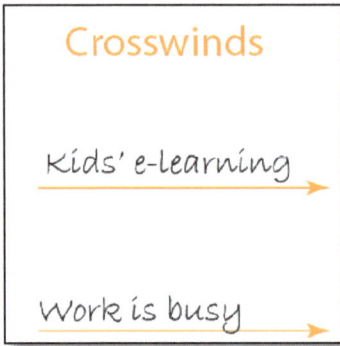

5. Likewise, you will want to identify Headwinds. These are anticipated obstacles to completing/progressing the Propeller πTask. Again, these may be the same each day or they may vary. The point is to think through the possible obstacles so that you recognize them and can respond appropriately. It is OK if these are unknown (or you run into one that you didn't anticipate.) Even writing "Unknown" in one of the lines is fine. The same benefits for preparing/anticipating Crosswinds apply to Headwinds too. Also, do not get hung up on whether something is a Crosswind (distraction) or a Headwind (obstacle). The entire purpose is anticipation and preparation; the semantics are absolutely unimportant.

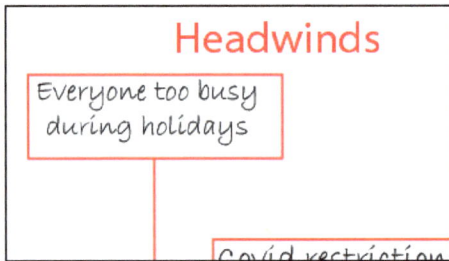

6. Finally, you also need to identify Tailwinds. These are external forces that will help you complete/progress the Propeller πTask for the day. They could be people (advocates, family members, delegates, or simply encouragers), solutions to some of the Crosswinds/Headwinds, or other systems/techniques to provide focus for your time/energy.

Call Phil for advice and encouragement		Tailwinds	Pray for people before calling them

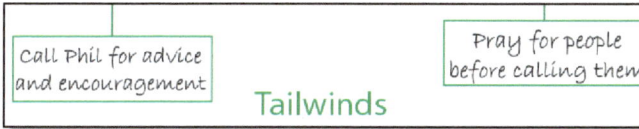

Once you have completed your daily Vector Modeling worksheet, use it to focus your time and energy on the πTask. When a Crosswind or Headwind pops up (because they will), jot it down if it was one you had not anticipated. Notice that the distractions and obstacles lose their power when they are anticipated. Rather than be blown off course, you can say, "Aha! I knew this (or something like it) was coming, and I know how to work through/around it." That's true even for the unknowns. They too have been anticipated and will not be able to deter you from your progress.

There is an example of a completed Vector Modeling worksheet on the next page.

πNautilus™ Vector Modeling™ Daily Worksheet

Focal πRoute:

Help 1 person
with piDest

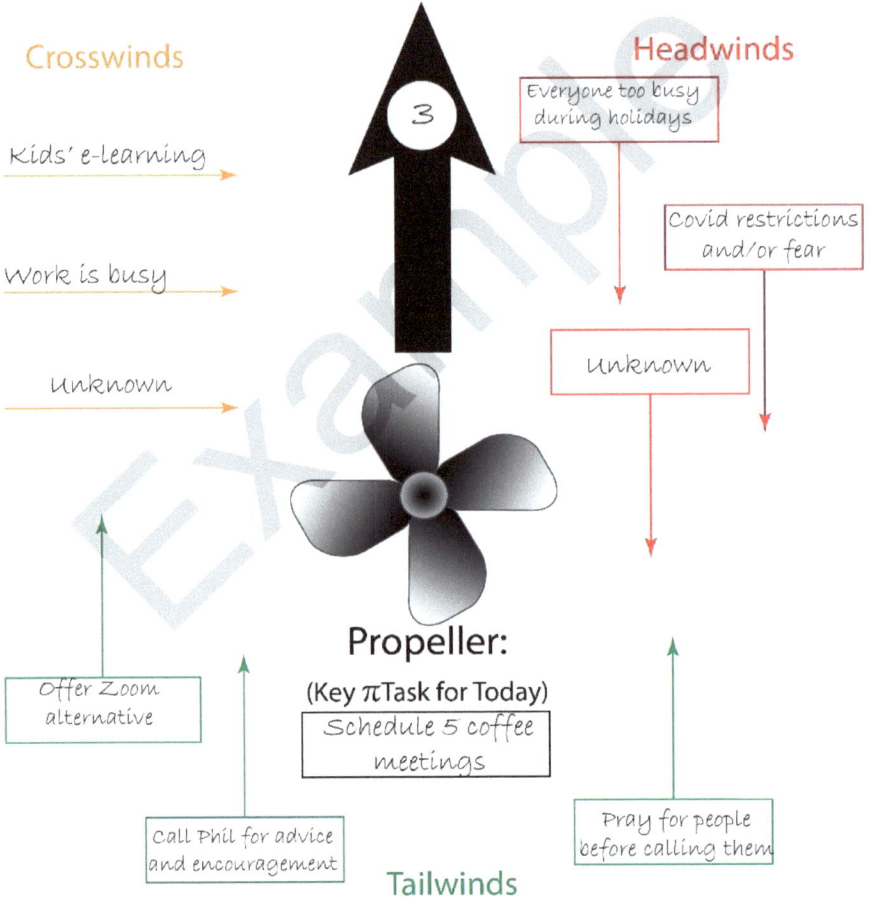

Crosswinds

Headwinds

3

Everyone too busy
during holidays

Kids' e-learning

Covid restrictions
and/or fear

Work is busy

Unknown

Unknown

Propeller:

(Key πTask for Today)

Schedule 5 coffee
meetings

Offer Zoom
alternative

Call Phil for advice
and encouragement

Pray for people
before calling them

Tailwinds

The πNautilus Vector Modeling Daily worksheet is in the previous section with the other worksheets. However, I recommend downloading the 8½ x 11 PDF version from www.piNautilus.com

About the Author

Sales trainer, business strategist, and Chief Navigational Officer of Greenfire Innovations, Eric Beschinski is passionate about simplifying the complexities in life and business. He has two decades of experience in the business world from employee to entrepreneur and account manager to sales trainer. Eric is a God-follower, a family guy, and a Renaissance man.

www.ingramcontent.com/pod-product-compliance
Lightning Source LLC
Chambersburg PA
CBHW051234090426
42740CB00001B/18